CONTENTS

LB BOOKS

Published 2024.
Little Brother Books Ltd, Ground Floor,
23 Southernhay East, Exeter, Devon, EX1 1QL
books@littlebrotherbooks.co.uk
www.littlebrotherbooks.co.uk
The Little Brother Books trademarks, logos,
email and website addresses, and the
GamesWarrior logo and imprint are sole and
exclusive properties of Little Brother Books Limited.
Printed in the United Kingdom.
Little Brother Books, 77 Camden Street Lower, Dublin, D02 XE80

THE HISTORY OF MARIO

The history of Mario as a character goes right back to Donkey Kong in 1981 - over 40 years ago. He wasn't even called Mario back then. Instead, he was called Jump Man. Mario was created by a Japanese game developer called Shigeru Miyamoto as a character who was trying to defeat Donkey Kong.

Since then, Mario has gone on to lead so many games it feels like there are too many to count! In 1985 Super Mario Bros. was released and featured lots of the things we now know Mario for, such as jumping in pipes, saving the princess and using power-ups.

MARIO 063250 ×49 WORLD 1-1 TIME

SUPER MARIO BROS.

©1985 NINTENDO

1 PLAYER GAME
2 PLAYER GAME

TOP- 063250

I·005710 TOP·005710

DUCK HUNT
ENTERTAINMENT SYSTEM
Nintendo
LIGHT GUN SERIES

He quickly became popular and came to be a mascot for the Nintendo company. He has since appeared in games across every single Nintendo console from the Nintendo Entertainment System (NES) all the way through handhelds and up to the Nintendo Switch.

IT'S-A ME, MARIO

Mario is a plumber who was once pulled into the Mushroom Kingdom and turned into a hero when he rescued the princess who was captured by an evil dragon. Sounds like a fairy tale - that's because Mario was based on classic myths and legends.

Mario is the shorter of the two brothers and always wears blue overalls with a red top. He always has a large bushy moustache, even when he transforms with a power-up.

Although he started out as a plumber, Mario has had lots of different jobs, including tennis player, footballer, racing driver, detective, musician and party planner.

PAPER MARIO

Paper Mario is a variant of the character who is completely 2D and is as flat as a sheet of paper. This version of Mario only appears in Paper Mario games, which are more like adventure games or RPGs than the usual platformers.

PAPER MARIO™

THE OTHER BROTHER, LUIGI

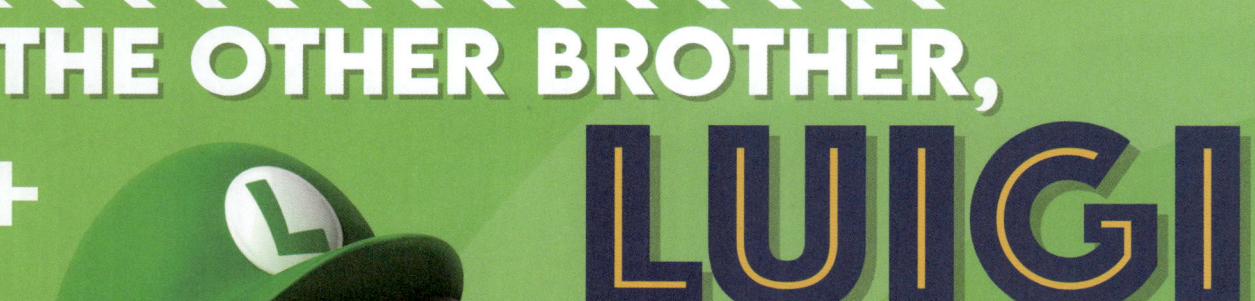

Luigi is taller than Mario and wears dark blue overalls with a green top rather than red. He was brought on this magical journey by his brother and they have since adventured in lots of different lands.

Luigi is very different to Mario, even though they look quite similar. For example, when Luigi jumps he often flutters his legs around making him float higher than Mario can.

Luigi has owned several mansions that always tend to be haunted, but he can defend himself with his ghost-busting vacuum cleaner. He has had three different adventures in haunted mansions, yet always ends up back in the same situation.

FUN FACT

When Luigi first appeared in Super Mario Bros. he was exactly the same as Mario in looks and ability. He was just a slightly green colour.

BABY LUIGI AND MARIO

Baby versions of the brothers have starred in a few games. Baby Mario first appeared in Yoshi's Island, trying to rescue his brother Luigi. The two baby versions also turned up in Mario Kart and are seen as cuter than the adult heroes.

TIME TO RESCUE THE
PRINCESS

Princess Peach is often the damsel in distress and must be saved by Mario and Luigi in many of the games. She has appeared in most of Mario's games in a number of ways and in more recent games, players can often choose to play as Peach.

Peach's favourite colour is pink and she is often seen wearing a long pink dress. She has shoulder length blonde hair and usually wears a golden crown. Nowadays, Peach is seen as a hero, rather than someone who always needs help.

Princess Peach is always kind and polite, she is also clever and loves an adventure. In the recent Super Mario Bros. movie, she is seen as very athletic and actually teaches Mario how move and fight.

FUN FACT

Peach was known as Princess Toadstool outside of Japan until the release of Super Mario 64. She is now known worldwide as Peach.

PRINCESS DAISY

Princess Daisy is Peach's best friend who wears yellow dresses and has darker hair. She first appeared in the Game Boy game Super Mario Land, taking the place of Peach. This was because the Game Boy game didn't take place in the Mushroom Kingdom and instead went to a land called Sarasaland. Since her first appearance, Daisy has been playable in many of the sports games and spin-offs.

TOADALLY TOAD +

Toad is one of the first characters players meet in Super Mario Bros. as he delivers the bad news that the princess is in a another castle, once you've beaten Bowser. Toad first appeared as a playable main character in Super Mario Bros. 2 where he featured along with Mario, Luigi and Princess Peach.

Toad is actually a unique member of the Toad species, who all look alike. If you've seen the Super Mario Bros. movie, you'll have seen that the Toad species live in the Mushroom Kingdom alongside Peach.

Toad has appeared in many games, including Mario Party and most of the sports games. He has also starred in his own game, Captain Toad, which was a puzzle game where players looked for treasure.

TOADETTE

Toadette is the female version of Toad and has appeared in several games more recently. She usually appears with a pink and white head that features two plaits at the sides. She wears a very similar waistcoat to toad, although hers is pink. She first turned up in Mario Kart: Double Dash and often accompanies Toad or Peach as a member of the Mushroom Kingdom.

YAY... IT'S YOSHI

An ally for our heroes, Yoshi is often a rideable character who adds new abilities for Mario or Luigi. He usually appears in his green form as he is the main member of the Yoshi race. A bit like the Toads, Yoshis are a race from the Mushroom Kingdom and they can be found in many different colours, including pink, black, white and blue.

Yoshi has appeared in many games, but he was first seen in Super Mario World and Yoshi's Island. He was actually named after the island because that's where his species was first discovered by Mario.

Yoshi is a dinosaur with a very long tongue and he loves gobbling down different items. He will lay eggs after eating fruits, even though Yoshi isn't female. These eggs often crack open to reveal a power-up or 1-Up mushroom. He can also gain new abilities after eating certain enemies.

COLOURFUL YOSHIS

Yoshi is already a powerful little guy because of his super stretchy tongue, but if he eats certain items he can gain powers. For example, eating a blue shell will allow him to fly, while eating a red shell means he can shoot three fireballs, and yellow shells can produce sand platforms to jump on. Of course, if it's a regular old green shell, then Yoshi can spit it out for the shell to travel along the ground and hit enemies.

1

IT'S ON... LIKE
DONKEY KONG

It all started with Donkey Kong. In his first game, he kidnapped a lady who Mario rescued by climbing platforms and collecting power-ups. After those original games Donkey Kong began appearing in more Mario games, and eventually, he got his own series on the SNES called Donkey Kong Country.

DK always wears his signature tie featuring his initials and his favourite food is bananas which he loves to gobble down on his home of Donkey Kong Island.

DK has started to appear in lots of Mario spin-off games, such as Mario Kart and Super Smash Bros. Donkey Kong can jump on the heads of his enemies, like Mario, but he can also tuck into a ball and launch himself forward, eliminating any bad guys in his way.

DIDDY AND DIXIE

Diddy Kong is the sidekick of DK and they're the best of friends. He first appeared alongside his friend in Donkey Kong Country. Diddy Kong once got his own racing game called Diddy Kong Racing. As the name suggests, Diddy is much smaller than DK.

Dixie is a female member of the Kong clan and is often seen in a pink hat and tied t-shirt. She has long blonde hair and is described as energetic and cheerful. She hasn't appeared in as many games as Diddy Kong, but she is a proud member of the family.

RADIANT ROSALINA

Rosalina is the newest princess to the Mario universe. She often appears in her long light-blue gown with a pendant and a silver crown. She has blonde hair that is much lighter than Peach's hair.

Rosalina will often be accompanied by a small star called Luma, who has been her best friend since she was a little girl lost in space. She first appeared in Super Mario Galaxy and her story was told throughout the game as the player collected more and more stars. It tells the story of Rosalina's mother going missing and Luma helping a young Rosalina find her family.

You can find Rosalina living in the Comet Observatory with lots of little Lumas. Rosalina is referred to as 'The Lady of the Shooting Stars' by Lubba, a large purple Luma who appears in Super Mario Galaxy 2.

LUMA

Lumas are star creatures. They look a bit like the power stars that Mario can collect, but these are happy little creatures who live with Rosalina and through outer space. They are powerful beings who can transform a planet into an entire galaxy. They see Rosalina as their mother and always call her 'mama.' Their name comes from the word 'lumen' which means light in the old language of Latin.

THE MIGHTY BOWSER +

Bowser is the leading enemy in the Super Mario games. He's mostly known as Bowser, but has also appeared as King Koopa or King Bowser. His favourite hobby seems to be kidnapping Princess Peach - he even forced her to marry him once - closely followed by fighting Mario. Bowser is the king of his own dark land where he rules over the Koopa Troop, a race of turtle-type creatures.

Although Bowser has the shell of a turtle, he can also breathe fire, which makes him more of a dragon. He has always been a nemesis of Mario since he first appeared in Super Mario Bros. back in 1985.

Bowser is known as being dangerous, but he is also very funny and often falls for his own traps. His goal is to defeat Mario and take over the Mushroom Kingdom. Although he is the bad guy, he is always invited to go karting, or join in with Mario Party games.

BOWSER JR

Sometimes known simply as Jr or Junior, Bowser's son will always help his father to kidnap Princess Peach. He first featured in Super Mario Sunshine where he appeared as 'Shadow Mario'. Bowser Jr always wants to make his dad proud so will fight Mario whenever he can. This little dragon is always very excited and can often make Bowser emotional, which is not how we normally see Bowser.

WA-WA-WARIO

As if Mario needed another rival, he met Wario in Super Mario Land 2: 6 Golden Coins on the GameBoy. Since then, Wario has been a nuisance for Mario and Luigi, but he has also become loved by the fans of the games.

Wario looks a bit like Mario, though everything looks a bit off compared to our hero. Wario has a big pink nose and a spiky moustache, plus his outfit is bright yellow. You can definitely tell the two apart, right? Over the years, Wario hasn't been bothering Mario as much, although they carry on their rivalry through Tennis, Karting and Party games.

Wario has appeared in a lot of Mario games, but he also has his own series of games. The Wario Land games were very similar to the platforms we see Mario running through. Plus Wario has a series called WarioWare that features lots of silly mini games.

WALUIGI

Waluigi is, obviously, Luigi's rival. Although he has never appeared as an enemy in the same way as Wario or Bowser. He first appeared in Mario Tennis, but since then he has become a fan favourite for his iconic "WAHHHHH" voiceline and his lanky height.
He's definitely not an evil enemy, but he's always up to no good.

EVIL ENEMIES

The Mario games have always had a big bad enemy controlling the story of the games, but Bowser, Wario and other bad guys have plenty of accomplices to help them battle Mario and Luigi.

KAMEK

This Koopa is a magician who flies around on a broomstick. He's the arch-enemy of Yoshi, but accompanies Bowser on many missions to defeat Mario and take over the Mushroom Kingdom.

BIRDO

Birdo is a dinosaur who was one of the main enemies in Super Mario Bros. 2. She fires eggs and fireballs from her mouth to hit our heroes. If a hero grabs an egg flying through the air, they can be thrown at Birdo to defeat her.

LAKITU

Lakitu is a Koopa with big goggles who travels inside a cloud. He throws out red spiny eggs that hatch into a spiny enemy that hurts Mario if he jumps onto it. Mario can leap onto Lakitu's head to knock him out of his cloud, which Mario can then travel in for a short time.

NABBIT

This rascally rabbit is always stealing items from our heroes, first appearing in Super Mario Bros. U as an enemy. In later games, Nabbit became a playable character who would make the game a little easier for younger players.

KING BOO

The leader of the Boos and the ghosts, this King is a friend of Bowser, often causing a nuisance in mansions within the Mario games. He also the main enemy of Luigi in the Luigi's Mansion games as he keeps kidnapping Mario!

BOWSER'S MINIONS

KOOPA

Koopas come in all shapes and sizes. Sometimes they have wings and they can appear in different colours, too, but Mario will always jump on them and use their shells as a weapon.

All good Mario games are filled with Bowser's minions - the small enemies that Mario has to defeat on the way to meet Bowser in the castles and floating ships of the games. These creatures have appeared in practically every single Mario game since the 1980s.

GOOMBA

These little grumpy mushroom dudes have been stomped by Mario for years. There's not much they can do to stop this as they aren't the toughest of enemies.

BOO

A Boo is a very shy ghost. If a hero looks at them the Boo will hide behind its hands and freeze in place. When the hero turns their back though, that's when a Boo will attack.

SPINY

Spinys can only be defeated by throwing a Koopa shell at them, or by using a Power Star which makes Mario invincible.

CHEEP CHEEP

These little fish live in the oceans of the Mushroom Kingdom. They sometimes leap from the water to attack Mario or Luigi, but they usually swim towards the heroes underwater to nip at their toes.

BOB-OMB

This little walking bomb can be used by Luigi to blow up other enemies, however they can also blow up in the faces of Mario or any other hero causing them a lot of damage.

BULLET BILL

Bullet Bills are fired from cannons and fly in a straight line. If they hit a hero they can cause damage, but they're pretty simple to jump on and eliminate.

WHERE TO PLAY

The Consoles

NINTENDO ENTERTAINMENT SYSTEM (NES)

The first mainstream console from Nintendo and the home of the very first Mario platformer. The controller was super simple with a directional control and only two buttons! The NES used large square cartridges which would hold the games information.

In Japan and America the NES and SNES had a very different name. They were called the Famicom and the Super Famicom. It was only with the N64 that the naming of the consoles became the same across the world.

SUPER NINTENDO ENTERTAINMENT SYSTEM (SNES)

Following on from the NES, the SNES doubled the first console's power, reduced the size of the game cartridges and gave players more control over the games with a better controller that featured four extra buttons. The console still mainly focused on 2D games.

NINTENDO 64 (N64)

Still using game cartridges, the N64 launched in 2001 and was the first fully 3D capable console from Nintendo. The controller now had a stick to control characters and featured even more buttons for actions to be performed. This console was home to the first 3D Mario adventure and, at the time, blew the minds of everyone who played.

GAMECUBE

This would be the first time Nintendo used discs for their games and introduced a second stick to the controller, which often controlled the cameras in games. It was a bit of an odd console as it used mini-CDs for the games, had a large carry handle bolted onto the back of the console and had four sockets for controllers, allowing four people to play at once.

Wii

Perhaps the most popular console of all-time, the Wii introduced motion controls which would be used in most of the games released. Each console was bundled with WiiSports which became one of the most popular games ever because everyone could play, whether young or old.

WiiU

The WiiU was perhaps the biggest mistake for Nintendo. The controller featured a large screen to accompany the TV or play games away from the console. It didn't sell very well and felt more like an experiment, which it kind of was.

NINTENDO SWITCH

Now Nintendo's best-selling console, the Switch took the WiiU idea of a screen in a controller, which developed into the handheld/home console that we know today. The Switch is a combination of everything that came before; it has motion controls, uses cartridges, and it has a large screen for games too. Mario Kart 8 Deluxe is the biggest selling video game on the Switch, selling over 52 million copies!

Nintendo has created several handheld consoles over the years, starting with the Game Boy. After this first handheld, we got the Game Boy Advance and the Nintendo DS and 3DS, which used two screens in a folding console.

GAMES

Mario has starred in a lot of games over the years. He spends most of his time trying to save his friends or family from his enemies. All this happens in games that we call 'platformers', where we control Mario running and jumping through different levels. These games are well-known in the history of Mario, and every fan should play if they haven't already.

SUPER MARIO BROS.

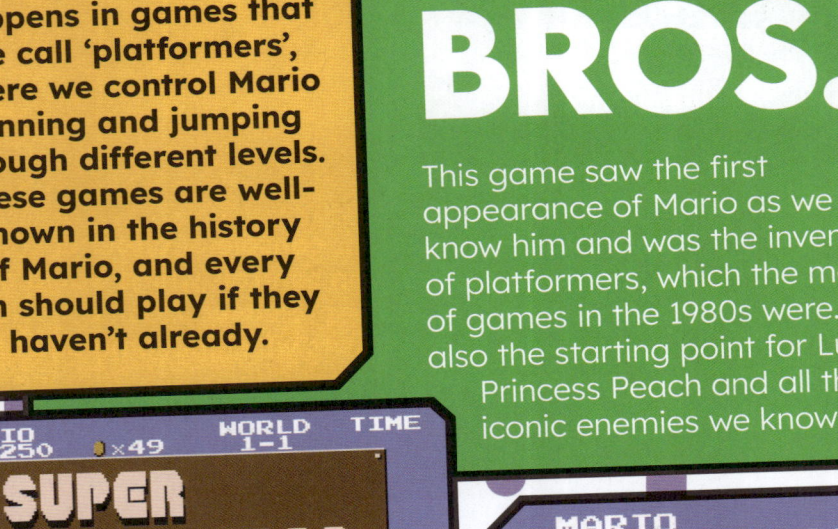

This game saw the first appearance of Mario as we now know him and was the invention of platformers, which the majority of games in the 1980s were. It was also the starting point for Luigi, Princess Peach and all the iconic enemies we know.

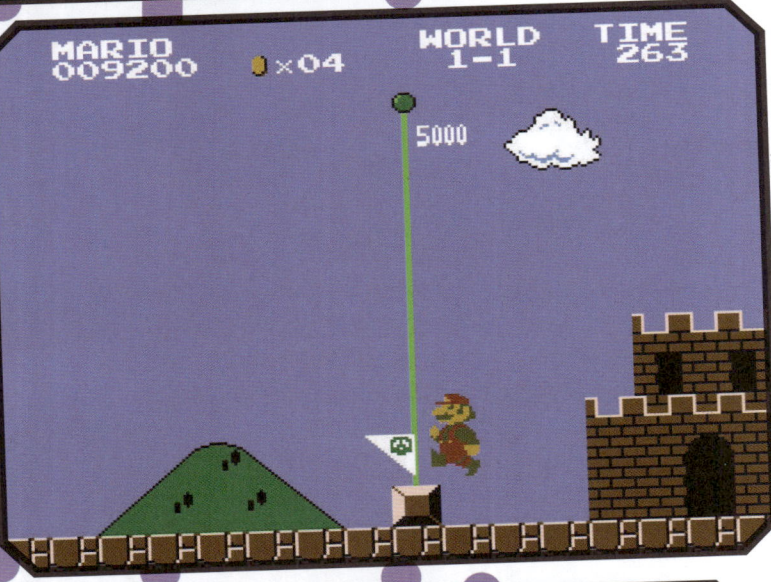

Before Super Mario Bros., video games weren't actually doing very well in the world and particularly in America. The popularity of Super Mario Bros. managed to save gaming and it became one of the most recognisable games ever created. This was a game that everyone wanted to play, from kids to grandparents - playing games on the family TV was a new occurrence and it captured so many people's attention.

This original game has been brought to an amazing number of consoles, including the NES, the SNES in the Mario All-Stars compilation game, all the way through to the Switch via the Switch Online catalogue.

SUPER MARIO BROS. 2

Super Mario Bros. 2 is an odd game in the history of Mario. Not only did it introduce four playable characters - Mario, Luigi, Peach and Toad - but it's not actually the second game in Japan, but the third. This sequel was created for America and Europe and completely changed the way Mario and friends would play.

JAPAN RELEASE

So why did Japan get a different game? The original sequel was Super Mario Bros.: The Lost Levels. This played and looked like the first game but was much harder to play. The difficulty was said to be too much for the American and European public, so Nintendo created what we now know as Super Mario Bros. 2. Eventually, Lost Levels would appear on Super Mario All-Stars on SNES.

In this game, Mario couldn't defeat enemies by jumping on their heads. By doing this, the character could pick up the enemy, hold them above their head, and throw them like a weapon. There were no Goombas, Koopas or enemies that players would recognise. It felt like a very different experience and became a game that many consider the worst of the series.

GAMES

SUPER MARIO BROS. 3

Super Mario Bros 3 took players back to a much more recognisable game. It looked a lot more like the first game, featured the traditional enemies and brought back eliminating enemies by jumping on their heads.

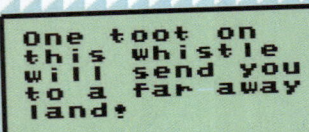
One toot on this whistle will send you to a far away land!

FUN FACT

This sequel was shown off in a movie called The Wizard. The film followed a kid who was amazing at video games and he reached the world finals of a competition where he would play Super Mario Bros. 3 and show off a couple of levels, plus the warp whistle, which transports players to other worlds in the game.

This third game introduced a lot of new features for Mario. Players could collect new power-ups, such as the frog suit which improved swimming and a feather which allowed Mario to fly, we could also now pick up Koopa shells to use them as weapons.

One major change was the overworld map which showed the upcoming levels, plus any bonus stages like fights with the Hammer Bros enemy who launched hammers at Mario, or the mini games where you could win extra lives.

SUPER MARIO WORLD

Jumping to a new console, the SNES, Mario kept the overworld map to show off levels, but also added more to the Mushroom Kingdom. Bowser introduced his Koopa kids plus a whole host of new enemies we'd never seen before. Who knew moles and flowers were so dangerous?!

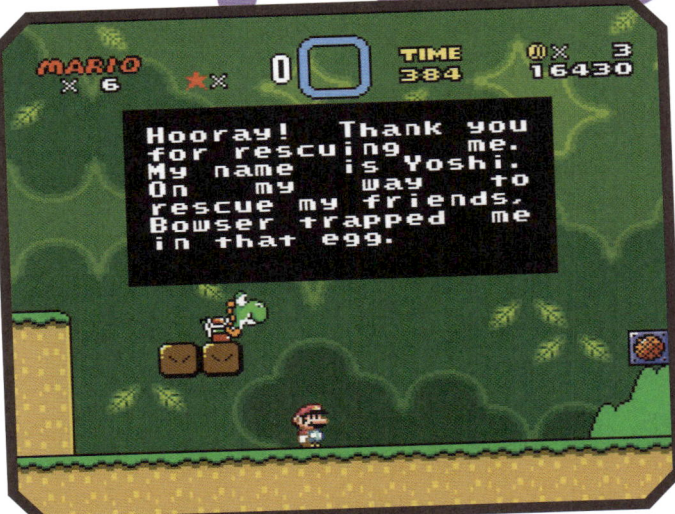

Of course, the most famous introduction in Super Mario World is everyone's favourite dinosaur, Yoshi. Yoshi could gobble up enemies or be used to reach high ledges. There were more ways to move around, including a cape for flying and a Power Balloon which filled Mario or Luigi with air so they could float.

Super Mario World introduced so many new enemies, characters, and items that it could fill this whole book! Let's take a deep breath and list a few... Dragon coins, Berries to be eaten by Yoshi, Springboards, P Switches that change level layouts, Dry Bones, Flying Koopas, Boo ghosts, a spin jump that protects Mario's feet, falling spikes, jumping piranha plants and spike traps.

KOOPA KIDS

The Koopa Kids are a group of seven Koopas who act as leaders of the Koopa species. They first appeared in this game to act as mini-bosses before Mario eventually gets to Bowser. Each of the Koopa Kids looks unique and has a special ability. Their names are; Iggy, Morton Koopa Jr, Lemmy, Ludwig Von Koopa, Roy, Wendy O. Koopa and Larry.

SUPER MARIO 64

This would be the first time Mario stepped into a 3D world and the traditional platforming was changed. Now players had to move in every direction, the obstacles and dangers had to change, but this also brought with it new ways to experience a Mario game.

Super Mario 64 is considered one of the best games ever made purely because of how it changed such an iconic hero. Now Mario would enter into worlds and have to collect a number of stars by completing missions, such as collecting eight red coins, or climbing to the high point of a world. In order to do this, Mario had a bunch of new ways to move. There was a total of 120 stars to collect.

Mario could now punch and kick enemies as well as jump on their heads; he could also triple jump, backflip, ground pound and long-jump. Each of these movements would be showcased in worlds or against certain enemies. From this point on, every Mario game seemed to bring a new feature and a bunch of new enemies, making each game feel unique.

Dear Mario:
Please come to the castle. I've baked a cake for you.
Yours truly--
Princess Toadstool

NEW CONTROLS

Super Mario 64 took advantage of the N64 and its new controller. Now Mario was meant to move within a 3D world, players needed a 3D stick to move him. The stick on the N64 controller could be pressed slightly to make Mario creep along and it made him spin in circles and become faster and more nimble.

SUPER MARIO SUNSHINE

In 2002, it was time for Mario to triple-jump over to another new console, the Gamecube. Super Mario Sunshine took Mario away from the Mushroom Kingdom and on holiday to Isle Delfino, which featured a whole new species called Piantas who were very colourful, and had trees growing from their heads and long noses.

resident of the Mushroom Kingdom. Data storage complete.

For this game, Mario had a kind of sidekick in FLUDD, a robotic backpack that could be filled with water that was used to fight, hover, solve puzzles and move around the worlds. As well as FLUDD, this game introduced Bowser Jr and more of the Toad species and brought Yoshi to the 3D games.

Much like Super Mario 64, the game was broken down into worlds where players would complete missions. Now you would be rewarded with a Shine Sprite, which looks like a golden coin shaped like a sun. Using Mario's new friend FLUDD, and his new movement tricks which used bursts of water, players could explore this beautiful tropical island.

FUN FACT

FLUDD stands for Flash Liquidiser Ultra Dousing Device and he happily chats away to Mario as they travel through each world.

GAMES

SUPER MARIO GALAXY

Super Mario Galaxy brought back the more familiar structure of players taking on levels one by one, rather than having a large world in which to complete missions. The twist here was that Mario and his friends were exploring space and each level was a planet, star or satellite. Many planets even had gravity that would alter how Mario moved.

Mario could now be controlled while he ran upside down underneath planets and could hop into pipes and appear within the core of a planet. There was a lot of flying and floating and some beautifully themed planets to explore. As well as featuring Princess Peach, this game contained the first appearance of Rosalina and the Luma species that would quickly become loved by fans.

This sequel is often considered the best Mario game in the long history because of how interesting each planet was, and how much it changed Mario's adventures.

SUPER MARIO GALAXY 2

Galaxy 2 was the first time Mario got a direct sequel game since the days of the NES classics. It didn't change a lot, but gave players more of what had come before, which was incredibly popular.

NEW SUPER MARIO BROS.

When Mario jumped onto the WiiU console there was a big change. Mario took the leap from 3D back to 2D and it felt more like retro Mario games, as we were side-scrolling again, but this game wanted lots of people to play together.

Super Mario Bros. U was designed for four people to play on the same screen, all bouncing off each other's heads and trying to reach the finish line of each level.

There was a new focus on Yoshi with this game and we got three baby Yoshis - blue, magenta and yellow. Each had a cool ability:

- **Blue** Yoshi could blow bubbles capturing enemies and turning them into coins or power-ups.
- **Magenta** Yoshi expanded like a balloon, it allowing players to jump higher and float along.
- **Yellow** Yoshi was a bright light bulb that could brighten dark areas.

NABBING NABBIT

Nabbit made his first appearance in Super Mario Bros. U. This character began popping up in levels players had completed, stealing items. By taking on the level containing Nabbit, the goal was to catch him before the level ended so you could win back the items.

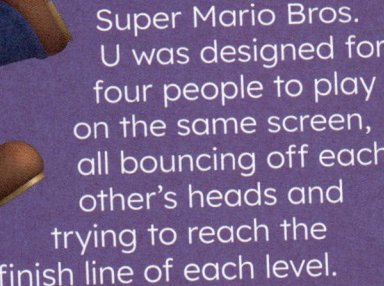

SUPER MARIO 3D WORLD

This release first launched for WiiU but it soon found a whole new audience on the Switch, and Mario kind of got back to his 3D adventures. You could play up to four players in a world that was 3D but viewed from an above angle. It's perhaps most famous for bringing in the cat suit, which turned Mario into a cat who could scratch at enemies or climb walls.

Super Mario 3D World introduced some really cool features, including the glass pipes which showed your character zooming through them. We also got to meet the Sprite princesses from Sprite Kingdom, who were desperate for Mario to help them defeat Bowser who kept capturing them in bottles.

This game also featured the first appearance of Captain Toad, who arrived in mini-levels where you had to guide him through a whole host of dangers in order to discover valuable treasure.

BOWSER'S FURY

When the game was rereleased for the Switch, a new smaller game called Bowser's Fury was included. In this game, Mario had to help Bowser Jr calm his father down otherwise Bowser would become Fury Bowser who could grow to be huge and start stomping all over the world of Lake Lapcat. Thankfully there were lighthouses and Giga Bells scattered around that helped to defeat Fury Bowser.

SUPER MARIO ODYSSEY

This game brings us to the latest Nintendo console, the Switch. Released early in the life of the new console, Super Mario Odyssey took us back to 'proper' 3D Mario and with it, a funny little sidekick called Cappy.

Cappy was the focus of Super Mario Odyssey. With his help, Mario could take control of any enemy or animal in the current level. This is seen in the very first level where Mario throws Cappy towards a T-Rex and suddenly starts to control the dinosaur, gobbling up little enemy creatures.

This game introduced a lot of new areas and enemies and also the ability to dress up Mario in cool outfits that matched the levels. Rather than finding stars in this game, we were finding moons which would power up our travelling airship allowing us to visit new worlds. Eventually the game took you to the moon for some ultra-difficult levels.

CALLING CAPPY

Cappy appeared in Odyssey, but they haven't popped up since. Hopefully, one day we'll see Cappy make a comeback in some way. The ability to control enemies was just so much fun and it left players wondering if there are any other Cappy creatures out in the world.

SUPER MARIO WONDER

We now find ourselves at the newest Mario game, which released for the Nintendo Switch in 2023. It marked a move back to 2D for Mario and his friends, while it combined lots of features from older games, including the overworld map and multiplayer through the game. Players could choose to use Mario, Luigi, Princess Peach and, for the first time, Princess Daisy.

Course clear!

You found a Wonder Seed!

ELEPHANTASTIC

Along with the wonder seeds, we got a brand new power-up that transformed Mario into an elephant. Not only did this transformation make Mario heavier, but he could also carry water in his trunk to put out fires or grow flowers in exchange for coins.

The big twist with Super Mario Wonder was the wonder seeds that made each level completely change. Sometimes the seeds turned everything black and white, or made green pipes come to life and inch across the ground like a worm. The seeds could even flip the levels upside down!

This game once again took our heroes to a new world. Mushroom Kingdom was left behind and we found ourselves in the Flower Kingdom, where a race of small caterpillar-like creatures lived. This world also brought shops and power-up abilities that could be changed before each level giving Mario different powers.

IT'S A WONDERFUL LIFE

Super Mario Wonder was a great game for bringing new abilities and features to the series. There was so much, that we couldn't fit it all on the last page! So, here are some of the best new additions from Super Mario Wonder.

LOTS OF CHARACTERS

You could choose Mario, Luigi, Peach, Daisy, Toad, Toadette and, for the first time ever, you could play as a Yoshi without a rider. Nabbit also made a comeback for younger players - if you use Nabbit he won't take damage from enemies.

BLOWING BUBBLES

Another new power-up for Wonder was the bubble flower, which allows Mario to throw bubbles at enemies and trap them.

TALKING FLOWERS

No characters speak in Super Mario Wonder besides sound effects like little yelps of joy. However, the flowers found throughout the levels do actually talk, which is brand new to this game.

DRILL MARIO

The last new power-up for Mario was the drill mushroom. This allows Mario to drill down into the ground, or jump below enemies and bop them with the pointy drill bit.

BADGES

For the first time, players could equip Mario with badges, each of which adds a new ability for Mario to use. Here are some of the best ones:

Parachute Cap - This lets you drift through the air after jumping.

Boosting Spin Jump - Press 'R' in mid-air to spin jump higher into the air.

Grappling Vine - Press 'R' in mid-air to shoot a beanstalk vine at a wall and use it as a grappling hook.

Safety Bounce - Bounce out of lava or bottomless pits.

Auto - You start every course with a super mushroom power-up.

SUPER QUIZ

Test your Super Mario knowledge. You'll find all the details you need for this quiz in this book.

1 What was Mario's original name in Donkey Kong?
- A Jump Man
- B Spin Man
- C Monkey Man

2 What is the name of Luigi's spin-off game?
- A Luigi's Bakery
- B Luigi's Mansion
- C Luigi's Hospital

3 Who does Mario save in most of the games?
- A Princess Pineapple
- B Princess Popcorn
- C Princess Peach

4 In which game did Yoshi first appear?
- A Super Mario World
- B Super Mario Planet
- C Super Mario Earth

5 What is the name of Rosalina's sidekick?
- A Luma
- B Looma
- C Louna

6 What object does Birdo shoot from her mouth?
- A Watermelon
- B Egg
- C Pumpkin

7 What colour is Wario's outfit?
- A Green
- B Black
- C Yellow

8 What's the name of Nintendo's first console?
- A MESS
- B NES
- C LESS

9 Which Nintendo console first introduced motion controls?
- A Wii
- B WiiU
- C Switch

10 How many copies of Mario Kart 8 Deluxe have been sold?
- A Over 32 million
- B Over 42 million
- C Over 52 million

11
Super Mario Bros. 3 introduced which power-up?
A Feather ⚪
B Cloud ⚪
C Acorn ⚪

12
Which is the real Koopa Kid?
A Morton ⚪
B Morris ⚪
C Mack ⚪

13
Mario first went 3D in which game?
A Super Mario 32 ⚪
B Super Mario 64 ⚪
C Super Mario 128 ⚪

14
What was the name of Mario's sidekick in Super Mario Sunshine?
A BLOOD ⚪
B MUDD ⚪
C FLUDD ⚪

15
Which of these isn't a Yoshi colour in Super Mario Bros U?
A Magenta ⚪
B Red ⚪
C Blue ⚪

16
Which is a real power-up in Super Mario 3D World?
A Cat ⚪
B Dog ⚪
C Mouse ⚪

17
What was the first Game Boy Mario game called?
A Super Mario Land ⚪
B Super Mario Ground ⚪
C Super Mario Earth ⚪

18
Where did the first Super Nintendo World theme park open?
A America ⚪
B Scotland ⚪
C Japan ⚪

19
Which sport DOESN'T Mario play?
A Football ⚪
B Tennis ⚪
C Rugby ⚪

20
Who created Mario?
A Satoru Iwata ⚪
B Shigeru Miyamoto ⚪
C Doug Bowser ⚪

HOW DID YOU SCORE?

0 - 5
Perhaps you need to go back to the Mushroom Kingdom.

6 - 10
You're gonna need a power-up.

11 - 15
You definitely know your Yoshi from your Toad.

16 - 19
You're a true Mario Super Star.

20!
You're a Super expert! Are you sure you didn't write this book?

ANSWERS ON PAGE 48

PICK UP A
POWER-UP

FIRE FLOWER

The Fire Flower puts the power of fire into Mario's hands and lets him shoot fireballs at enemies. One fireball usually kills smaller enemies, but it will take more to finish larger baddies.

If Mario is known for one thing, it's usually the power-ups he collects that transform his body. The very first power-up available to players in Super Mario Bros. was the Super Mushroom that grows Mario from his small form to his bigger form.

CANNON BOX

This hat is found in Super Mario World and Mario Maker. While wearing the Cannon Box, the cannon continually shoots cannonballs that kill enemies or break walls.

MEGA MUSHROOM

Mario is able to collect this power-up in several games and it makes him grow into a huge version of himself, stomping enemies, blocks and everything in his way.

ICE FLOWER

Completely the opposite to Fire Flower, this one shoots balls of ice that freeze enemies. Once frozen they can be broken by jumping on their heads.

DOUBLE CHERRY

This Cherry power-up from Super Mario 3D World multiplies Mario, creating copies of him that move along with the original. It is often used to solve puzzles.

BEE MUSHROOM

Found in Super Mario Galaxy, the Bee Mushroom transforms Mario into a bee and let's him fly for short periods of time.

SUPER STAR

Collecting the Super Star makes Mario invincible, meaning he doesn't take any damage from enemies and he can kill them by running into them.

BONUS GAMES

These extra Mario games come from different consoles, like the handhelds Nintendo has made famous over the years. They're considered an important part of the history of Mario.

SUPER MARIO LAND

When Nintendo released the Game Boy, which was its first handheld console, they wanted to launch a Mario game with it. The console didn't have as much power as the home consoles, and it had a green and black screen. This made Mario and the world of Sarasaland look very tiny and less colourful than normal.

As this was such a different Mario experience, it deserved a new princess for Mario to rescue, introducing Princess Dasiy. Because this was a different world, many of Mario's familiar enemies didn't appear and instead, we had all new enemies to defeat.

PORTABLE PLATFORM

Since the release of Super Mario Land, Mario has appeared in over 15 different platforming games and over 140 handheld games.

This game was very successful and Super Mario Land became one of the best-selling titles for the Game Boy. It was so popular that it got several sequels, the second of which introduced Wario and Mario even had his own castle!

SUPER MARIO MAKER 1 & 2

Both of the Super Mario Maker games were a great chance for fans to do something they never had before - to create their own Mario games. Both of these games made creating Mario levels really easy by selecting items and dropping them into a blank canvas. Even better, players could share their creations with the world.

Players began to make some brilliant levels. Some recreated genres like 'escape rooms', others were simple, more traditional levels, while others were prone to being super difficult. It was really easy to find levels you were interested in via the search function, or you could play random levels.

Eventually, certain creators began to stand out for creating levels as good as anything that Nintendo would make themselves. Between the two games, several game modes kept you playing, particularly the 'endless challenge' which meant having to play as many levels as possible before Mario lost all his lives.

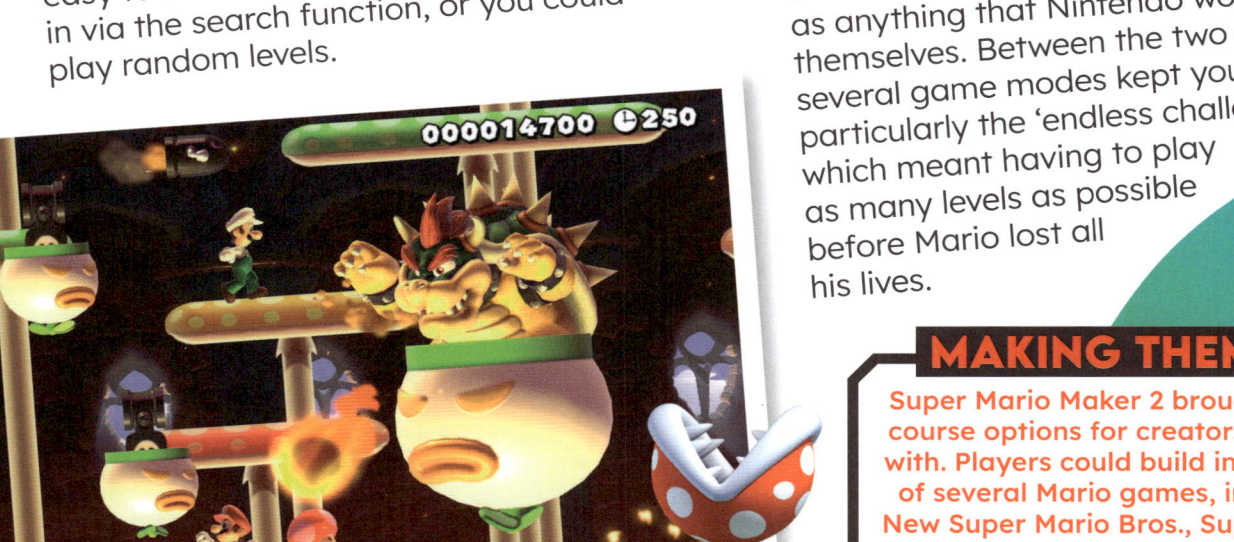

MAKING THEMES

Super Mario Maker 2 brought more course options for creators to build with. Players could build in the style of several Mario games, including New Super Mario Bros., Super Mario Bros., Super Mario 3D World, Super Mario World and Super Mario Bros. 3.

BONUS GAMES

SUPER MARIO KART

HISTORY

The Mario Kart games were a bit of a strange change for Mario and his friends. Nobody expected Mario to jump from platforms and side-scrolling games into kart racing. The first Mario Kart game released for the SNES in 1992. It was so incredibly successful it not only got a bunch of sequels, but also spawned so many other karting games from other video games companies.

When including all platforms, there have been over 14 Mario Kart games! This includes five home console games, three portable games for handheld consoles, a mobile game which recently stopped development, and four arcade games released worldwide.

The games are simple and addictive; players race against each other, or against bots, across a number of laps, collecting weapons and items on the tracks that can be used against each other. There's also a dedicated multiplayer mode where players must use weapons to pop balloons that surround karts - when all balloons are popped your racer is outof the game.

DIFFERENT RACERS

Everybody has their favourite character to race as. Some will pick the cute and cuddly Yoshis or Toads, while others choose the bad guys of Bowser or the Koopa Kids. What not many people know is that the racers are broken down into weights:

Smaller characters are lightweights who have faster acceleration.

Medium size characters are great all rounders.

Large characters can easily knock others aside but suffer lower acceleration.

50cc
100cc
150cc
Mirror
200cc

← B

CRAZY FAST! Braking is cruc

Ⓐ OK

Mario Kart 8 is the most recent entry into the Mario Kart franchise. It was originally released for WiiU in 2014, before being released a second time for the Nintendo Switch as Mario Kart 8 Deluxe. It is the best-selling Mario Kart game of all time and recently got bigger than ever with a bunch of new courses to download.

There were a lot of new things introduced in Mario Kart 8 including anti-gravity sections in tracks where players could ride on the ceilings or walls. This was the first karting game to bring in lots of new characters, such as Baby Rosalina, Wiggler, Piranha Plant and more. It also included characters from other great Nintendo games like Zelda and Animal Crossing.

BOOSTER COURSE PASS

For a long time, players didn't expect to see any new tracks for Mario Kart 8 Deluxe, but they were surprised when Nintendo announced the Booster Course Pass which eventually brought 48 new and improved courses to the game. This brought the total number of courses to 96! The courses included came from past games, the Mario Kart mobile game, and all new courses created by Nintendo. Along with the new courses, we also got a few new characters, including Birdo, Petey Piranha, Wiggler, Kamek, Diddy Kong, Funky Kong, Pauline and Peachette.

YOSHI'S ISLAND

MARIOKART
MIX-UPS

In this mixed up Mario page, we've got a bunch of jumbled anagrams for you to solve. Each one is the name of a character

1 MRAIO

2 SAYDI

3 ROBDI

4 ASOILRAN

5 YOIHS

6 IWLAIGU

7 ROWSBE

8 DIGWLU

9 RWOAI

10 YWDNE

11 UKLITA

12 REIWGGL

ANSWERS ON **PAGE 48**

MARIO'S FUN FACTS

Did you know that Mario was not originally going to be a plumber? He was supposed to be a carpenter.

Donkey Kong Jr, a sequel from 1982, is the only game where Mario plays the bad guy. In this game he has trapped Donkey Kong in a cage.

The chain chomp enemy in the games is inspired by a ferocious dog who would bark at the creator of Mario when he was little.

Before the recent Super Mario Bros. animated movie, there was another film in 1993. It was pretty much disliked by everyone and considered a huge failure.

Did you know that Mario has appeared in over 200 different video games?!

Yoshi isn't actually Yoshi's full name. His name is apparently T. Yoshisaur Munchakoopas.

The only reason Mario wears a hat is because it was too difficult to program hair back in the 1980s.

Bowser was originally supposed to be an ox. However, when it came to drawing him, artist Yoichi Kotabe misunderstood and drew a turtle.

SUPER MARIO BROS.
MOVIE

In 2023 Nintendo teamed up with Illumination studio and Universal Pictures to create a movie called The Super Mario Bros. Movie. It was the second attempt at making a Mario Bros. film and it was incredibly successful compared to the first try.

In the latest film, Mario stumbles across a pipe that leads him to the Mushroom Kingdom where he meets Princess Peach and the Toad species. As the hero, Mario has to rescue Luigi from Bowser and stop him from taking over the world. It was a bright and colourful film that many Mario fans had waited years to see.

The film was incredibly successful making over $1 billion, holding the record for the highest-selling video game movie of all time. In many Eastern countries, the film was released on Mario day which, if you didn't know, is on March 10th because the month and date spell out MAR10.

SUPER NINTENDO WORLD
JAPAN

It was a long time coming but in 2020, despite the worldwide pandemic, Nintendo opened Super Nintendo World in Japan's Universal Studios theme park. The new area of the park essentially dropped visitors into Mario's world, the Mushroom Kingdom, as we've known it for years.

On display were huge green pipes, mushroom houses, piranha plants and castles. There were even blocks hovering in the air, just as they would for Mario. Everything looked just like it would in the games and fans loved it, making it incredibly popular.

The park features many moments from Mario history, including a Mario Kart ride, a chance to ride Yoshi through a short adventure and a bunch of mini attractions dedicated to the characters we know and love.

GOING TO HOLLYWOOD

The success of the theme park meant that more Universal theme parks around the world started building their own versions of Super Nintendo World. The next to open was in America, in Hollywood, in fact. And as of right now, a version is being built in Singapore.

SUPER SPORTY

Over the years, Mario and his friends have appeared in a lot of sports games. These include tennis, golf, baseball and football. He also teamed up with his once rival, Sonic the Hedgehog, for the Olympic Games crossovers.

Mario's first sports game was Mario Golf on the SNES, though it wasn't that popular to start with. It was only when the N64 released that these sports games started to become popular with players and Mario began branching out to new sports.

There have been around 55 different games dedicated to sports. The sports are usually those that are most popular in Japan and America, which is why baseball appears a few times. The Olympics and Winter Olympics have been the most successful, particularly on the Wii as its motion controls were perfect for representing different sports, such as javelin, hammer throw and sprint, where players had to shake the controller to run.

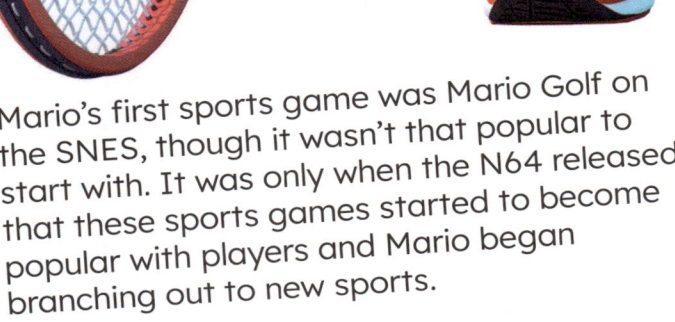

TEAMMATES

For many years, Nintendo had a friendly rivalry with another console developer, SEGA. Many would side with Mario and Nintendo, while others chose SEGA and Sonic the Hedgehog. Eventually the rivalry died off when SEGA stopped producing consoles in the early 2000s. This led to Sonic and Mario teaming up in 2007 for the first Olympic Games title.

POWER-UP
WORDSEARCH

We've thrown a bunch of Mario power-ups and items into this mixed up grid for you to spot. Can you find all the words and become a Mario Super Star?

H	G	C	M	M	C	G	H	Z	A	D	Z	B	B	H
F	A	E	L	R	U	G	N	G	I	U	A	O	A	W
R	C	B	O	G	H	S	N	I	I	M	Z	O	L	S
L	I	W	W	F	B	X	H	V	W	M	C	M	L	X
G	N	T	N	D	T	I	H	R	U	N	R	E	O	S
L	O	D	U	D	A	Z	A	J	O	A	Z	R	O	T
K	L	O	S	D	M	C	L	F	T	O	T	A	N	B
Q	L	E	U	U	Q	F	O	S	B	Z	M	N	X	U
C	J	H	H	B	E	L	L	R	F	B	I	G	F	R
T	E	E	H	S	V	V	Y	X	N	I	C	E	Z	E
L	G	U	D	Y	E	Z	P	T	B	N	A	Y	Z	M
U	X	U	K	U	J	J	A	B	P	T	Y	F	I	M
Y	R	R	E	H	C	H	S	P	H	B	U	M	G	A
G	F	L	O	W	E	R	K	E	A	V	L	Y	F	H
U	N	B	P	B	Z	K	R	V	J	L	J	G	U	F

STAR • FLOWER • MUSHROOM • FEATHER • BOOMERANG

CHERRY • SHELL • HAMMER • CLOUD • BELL

ACORN • BALLOON • CROWN • LEAF • WING

ANSWERS ON PAGE 48

41

IT'S SMASH TIME

Super Smash Bros. is another of those games that nobody would have expected Nintendo to create. Until this point, they'd never made any fighting games, but there was definitely a group of people who wanted the chance to punch and kick some of Nintendo's well-loved cast. Super Smash Bros., with every edition, became one of the company's best-selling games.

If you've never played one of these games, the idea is to control a character and, using a range of special moves, beat the other players by knocking them off the level map. The centre of each map is a set of platforms with a bottomless pit on either side. If you fall in the pit, or get knocked off the screen, it's game over.

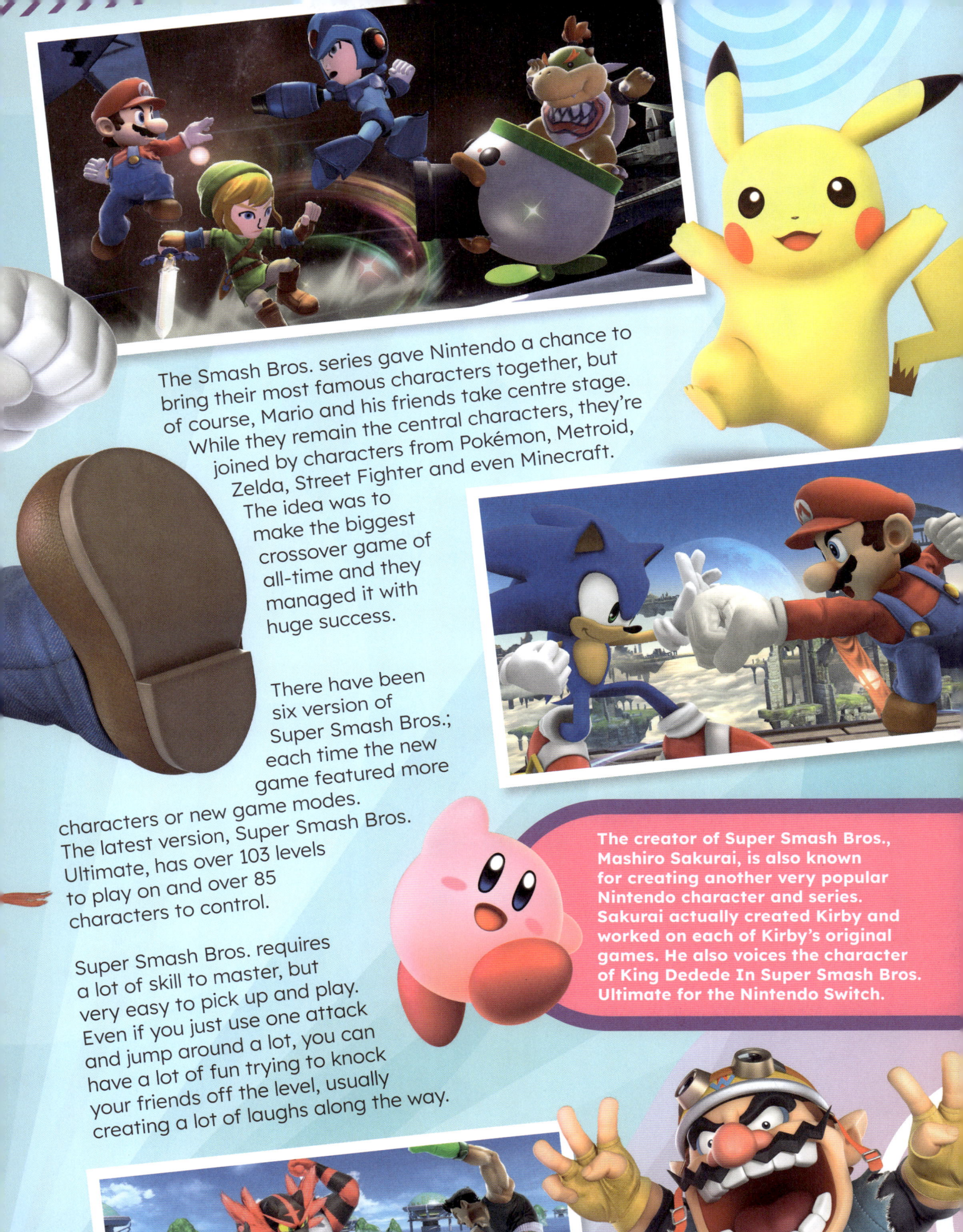

The Smash Bros. series gave Nintendo a chance to bring their most famous characters together, but of course, Mario and his friends take centre stage. While they remain the central characters, they're joined by characters from Pokémon, Metroid, Zelda, Street Fighter and even Minecraft. The idea was to make the biggest crossover game of all-time and they managed it with huge success.

There have been six version of Super Smash Bros.; each time the new game featured more characters or new game modes. The latest version, Super Smash Bros. Ultimate, has over 103 levels to play on and over 85 characters to control.

Super Smash Bros. requires a lot of skill to master, but very easy to pick up and play. Even if you just use one attack and jump around a lot, you can have a lot of fun trying to knock your friends off the level, usually creating a lot of laughs along the way.

The creator of Super Smash Bros., Mashiro Sakurai, is also known for creating another very popular Nintendo character and series. Sakurai actually created Kirby and worked on each of Kirby's original games. He also voices the character of King Dedede In Super Smash Bros. Ultimate for the Nintendo Switch.

LET'S GET THIS MARIO PARTY STARTED!

The Mario Party series is the perfect game for families and friends. Each game is a board game, a bit like Monopoly; you and your chosen players roll a dice to move around a board collecting coins, power-ups and stars. The person with the most stars at the end of the game wins. But there's a brilliant catch to it...

Mario Party is all about minigames. Silly little games where you mash the buttons as fast as you can, or control your character through a maze, or spot differences in scenes. Throughout the 12 Mario Party games there have been hundreds of minigames. In some you work as a team, in others the game can be won by anybody. These games sometimes require skill, but a lot of the time are based on luck or how well you work with another player.

All the game boards are themed and are based on worlds we've seen in Mario games over the years. They always feature cute characters who can change how a board plays, by adding shortcuts or removing scenery - sometimes they can give out items to help in games or punish you by taking away coins which you'd normally use to buy items.

You can often set your own rules for each game, plus set a time limit too. So if you only have 30 minutes to play, you can set the timer and the game will end after 30 minutes are up. This is a brilliant game to play with your friends and family. Plus, a lot of the minigames are super silly and so much fun.

If you just want to play the minigames, you can certainly do that. You don't have to work your way around the boards. If you and your friends want to, you can mess around on the minigames and see who is the best at each one.

Peach's Birthday Cake

You Got a Star!

There have been 12 Mario Party games, which includes two for Nintendo Switch. Also, if you're a member of Nintendo Switch Online, you can access many of the older games through the N64 system feature, where you can play older games for free.

THE WEIRD AND WONDERFUL

There have been several weird and wonderful games in Mario's past; games that were very unexpected, but saw a lot of success.

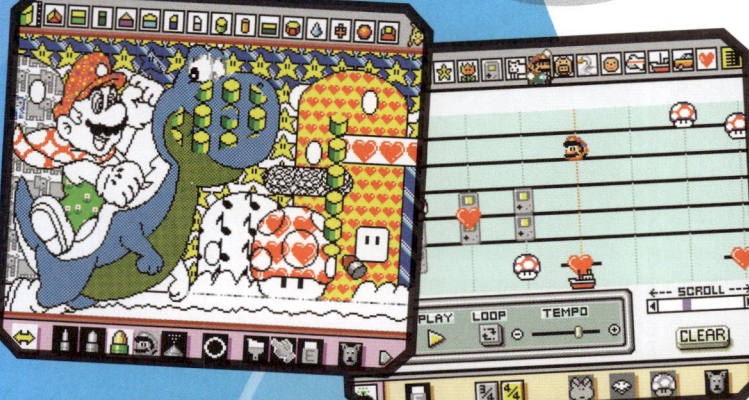

SUPER MARIO RPG

Role Playing Games are an incredibly popular genre of games, particularly in Japan, where Nintendo is based. Because of this, Nintendo wanted to create a Mario RPG with a long and deep story as well as a new way to combat enemies. The first Mario RPG released for the SNES and has recently been remade for the Nintendo Switch.

MARIO PAINT

One of these games was Mario Paint, which appeared on the SNES. It was a painting game that taught players how to draw various Mario characters using a painting program. It also featured a music maker where people could make songs using the sound effects from the Mario games.

GAME AND WATCH

The Game and Watch toys were some of the earliest Nintendo games. These were small handheld electronic games with animated graphics playing over a painted background. You couldn't change the games like with the Game Boy or Nintendo Switch, instead each handheld contained one game. Many of these released in 1982 and featured Mario or Donkey Kong.

DR MARIO

After the huge success of Tetris on Game Boy, Nintendo wanted to find the next best puzzle game, and they wanted Mario to take part. What followed was Dr Mario, a game where players would drop colourful medication and pair up the colours. These pairings and chain reactions would then kill off horrible germs and illnesses that looked like monsters.

MIYAMOTO & MARIO

It's worth taking some time to meet the man who created Mario; a man who has worked for Nintendo since 1977 and is responsible for many of the games you love. Shigeru Miyamoto (pronounced Shee-ga-roo Mee-ah-mo-toe) started working for Nintendo early on in his career of making games. He was the director for Donkey Kong where he created Mario to appear.

Miyamoto went on to create the Mario Bros. series as we know it today and has worked on many of the mainline Mario platforms, whether in 3D or 2D. He is also listed as directing, producing or creating several other popular Nintendo titles, including Kid Icarus, The Legend of Zelda, F-Zero, Pokémon Red and Blue, Pikmin, Nintendogs, Wii Sports and Metroid Prime. He has also been a supervisor on most of Nintendo's consoles.

His legacy is not only important to Nintendo, but to all video games. Without Shigeru Miyamoto and his imagination, there are many games that wouldn't exist today.

ANSWERS

28-29 - SUPER MARIO QUIZ

1. A, Jumpman
2. B, Luigi's Mansion
3. C, Princess Peach
4. A, Super Mario World
5. A, Luma
6. B, Egg
7. C, Yellow
8. B, NES
9. A, Wii
10. C, Over 52 million
11. A, Feather
12. A, Morton
13. B, Super Mario 64
14. C, FLUDD
15. B, Red
16. A, Cat
17. A, Super Mario Land
18. C, Japan
19. C, Rugby
20. B, Shigeru Miyamoto

36 - MARIO KART MIX-UPS

1. Mario
2. Daisy
3. Birdo
4. Rosalina
5. Yoshi
6. Waluigi
7. Bowser
8. Ludwig
9. Wario
10. Wendy
11. Lakitu
12. Wiggler

41 - POWER-UP WORDSEARCH

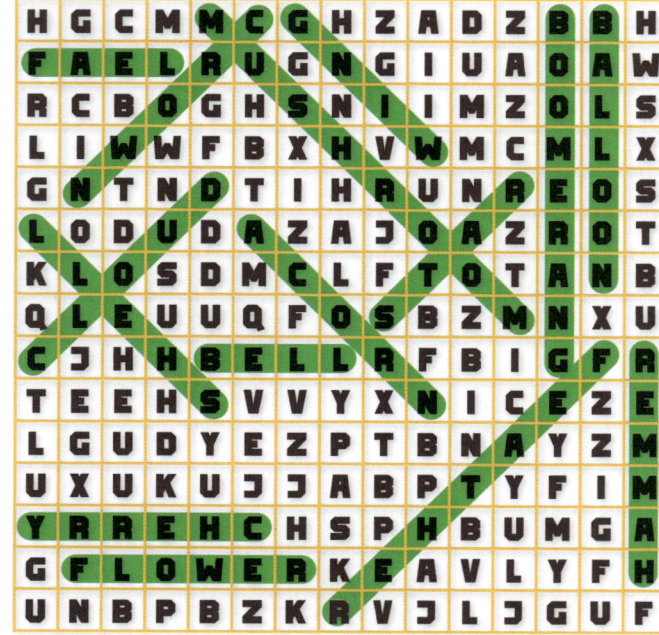